T0049226

EXPERIMENTING WITH
Science

by Olivia J. Mullins, PhD

Founder of Science Delivered

WILEY

EXPERIMENTING WITH SCIENCE

Published by:
John Wiley & Sons, Inc.,
111 River Street, Hoboken,
NJ 07030-5774,

www.wiley.com

Copyright © 2016 by John Wiley & Sons, Inc., Hoboken, New Jersey

Published simultaneously in Canada

No part of this publication may be reproduced, stored in a retrieval system or transmitted in any form or by any means, electronic, mechanical, photocopying, recording, scanning or otherwise, except as permitted under Sections 107 or 108 of the 1976 United States Copyright Act, without the prior written permission of the Publisher. Requests to the Publisher for permission should be addressed to the Permissions Department, John Wiley & Sons, Inc., 111 River Street, Hoboken, NJ 07030, (201) 748-6011, fax (201) 748-6008, or online at http://www.wiley.com/go/permissions.

Trademarks: Wiley, For Dummies, Dummies.com, and related trade dress are trademarks or registered trademarks of John Wiley & Sons, Inc. and may not be used without written permission. All other trademarks are the property of their respective owners. John Wiley & Sons, Inc. is not associated with any product or vendor mentioned in this book.

LIMIT OF LIABILITY/DISCLAIMER OF WARRANTY: THE PUBLISHER AND THE AUTHOR MAKE NO REPRESENTATIONS OR WARRANTIES WITH RESPECT TO THE ACCURACY OR COMPLETENESS OF THE CONTENTS OF THIS WORK AND SPECIFICALLY DISCLAIM ALL WARRANTIES, INCLUDING WITHOUT LIMITATION WARRANTIES OF FITNESS FOR A PARTICULAR PURPOSE. NO WARRANTY MAY BE CREATED OR EXTENDED BY SALES OR PROMOTIONAL MATERIALS. THE ADVICE AND STRATEGIES CONTAINED HEREIN MAY NOT BE SUITABLE FOR EVERY SITUATION. THIS WORK IS SOLD WITH THE UNDERSTANDING THAT THE PUBLISHER IS NOT ENGAGED IN RENDERING LEGAL, ACCOUNTING, OR OTHER PROFESSIONAL SERVICES. IF PROFESSIONAL ASSISTANCE IS REQUIRED, THE SERVICES OF A COMPETENT PROFESSIONAL PERSON SHOULD BE SOUGHT. NEITHER THE PUBLISHER NOR THE AUTHOR SHALL BE LIABLE FOR DAMAGES ARISING HEREFROM. THE FACT THAT AN ORGANIZATION OR WEBSITE IS REFERRED TO IN THIS WORK AS A CITATION AND/OR A POTENTIAL SOURCE OF FURTHER INFORMATION DOES NOT MEAN THAT THE AUTHOR OR THE PUBLISHER ENDORSES THE INFORMATION THE ORGANIZATION OR WEBSITE MAY PROVIDE OR RECOMMENDATIONS IT MAY MAKE. FURTHER, READERS SHOULD BE AWARE THAT INTERNET WEBSITES LISTED IN THIS WORK MAY HAVE CHANGED OR DISAPPEARED BETWEEN WHEN THIS WORK WAS WRITTEN AND WHEN IT IS READ.

For general information on our other products and services, please contact our Customer Care Department within the U.S. at 877-762-2974, outside the U.S. at 317-572-3993, or fax 317-572-4002. For technical support, please visit https://hub.wiley.com/community/support/dummies.

Wiley publishes in a variety of print and electronic formats and by print-on-demand. Some material included with standard print versions of this book may not be included in e-books or in print-on-demand. If this book refers to media such as a CD or DVD that is not included in the version you purchased, you may download this material at http://booksupport.wiley.com. For more information about Wiley products, visit www.wiley.com.

Library of Congress Control Number: 2016943664

ISBN: 978-1-119-29133-6 (pbk); ISBN 978-1-119-29135-0 (ePDF); ISBN 978-1-119-29134-3 (epub)

Manufactured in the United States of America

10 9 8 7 6 5 4 3 2 1

CONTENTS

INTRODUCTION

WELCOME TO EXPERIMENTING WITH SCIENCE. I am so excited to guide you in your scientific journey as you test, explore, learn, have fun, and, yes, experiment. My goal is for you to experience the thrill of scientific discovery.

SO WHAT IS SCIENCE? Science is the study of the world around you — or even the world inside of you. In this book, you learn about many scientific disciplines, so get ready to make some reactions, trick your brain, harness magnetic forces, combine science and art, and more!

ABOUT SCIENTISTS

Scientists are so diverse it's hard to know how to describe them. In research laboratories (where scientists work), you will find men and women, young and old, from countries all over the world. But all scientists have one thing in common: They love learning and have a big curiosity about how the world works.

The job of a scientist is to discover new things, and they study all sorts of different stuff. Some scientists study how to cure diseases in hopes of helping people stay healthy. Some study gigantic collapsing stars, while others study the behavior of tiny ants. For some scientists, it's normal to scuba dive around the ocean taking video of elusive sea creatures. It's safe to say that scientists have pretty cool jobs.

If you're a person who is curious about the world, you may consider being a scientist when you grow up.

ABOUT THIS BOOK

This book is filled with fun and enlightening science experiments. The experiments are split up into seven chapters, and each chapter starts with a quick introduction and a section about the science behind the experiments (with the exception of the final chapter). The best thing to do is to read this science overview before starting the experiments within the chapter. Don't worry if you don't understand everything at once. Learning about science is a process that can take time.

Each chapter contains several experiments. You don't have to do the experiments in order or even do all of them, although sometimes it may be helpful to complete some of the earlier, simpler experiments first.

Each experiment starts with a brief description of what you will be doing and a supply list. Make sure that you have all the supplies you need before you get started. (You can find most supplies around the house or at a grocery store. A few experiments have slightly more specialized supplies that you may need to order.) You can find a master supply list at www.dummies.com/go/experimentingwithscience.

You can then follow the instructions to start your project. While you're working, make sure that you make observations of what you see, hear, feel, or even smell! I encourage you to make predictions of what you think will happen in your experiment. If you want to keep track of your predictions and data, go online to www.dummies.com/go/experimentingwithscience to find guidelines for making your own lab notebook.

When you complete your experiment, read about the science at the end of each project. This information helps you understand what you just observed. Some of these concepts are pretty crazy! See whether the explanations are consistent with your observations and experimental results.

At the end of each experiment is a section that tells you how you can take the experiment further. This is a very important section! Science is all about curiosity and discovery. You can usually do an experiment in more than one way, and you can expand on the experiments presented in the book in a lot of ways. I encourage you to use the projects and instructions outlined in the book as a starting point and then go wild. Follow your curiosity and don't be limited by the steps on the page.

As you go through the book, some experiments will work immediately, but some may take a couple tries. Don't worry if you have to try the experiment a few times. It turns out that every scientist has had many experiments that don't work. In fact, you often learn just as much, or more, from what goes wrong as you learn from what goes right. But you learn the most when you're enjoying what you do, so start experimenting and have a blast!

SAFETY

Safety is a very important part of science. Do not eat or drink your experiments. Do not rub your eyes if you have chemicals on your hands. Something like lemon juice is mostly safe, but it will sting a whole lot if you get it in your eyes! Pay attention to any safety warnings I have on the experiments and wear gloves and eye protection when necessary.

ABOUT YOU

You are a wonderful, bright, and curious kid. Maybe you already love science, or maybe you aren't so sure if you like it. Maybe school is easy for you, or maybe sometimes it's really tough! Either way, science is for all kids, and the experiments in this book are for you.

WHAT YOU NEED TO KNOW

One thing you need to know for many experiments in this book is how to make measurements. If you're unsure how to measure out things like 8 inches or ½ tablespoon, it's no problem – just find an adult to help you out with this part.

ABOUT THE ICONS

As you read through the projects in this book, you'll see a few icons. The icons point out different things:

This icon points out tips that can make your experiments run more smoothly.

This icon alerts you to information that you'll want to remember.

Pay attention to the warnings! They contain safety information or instructions on how to perform an experiment without damaging anything in your house (like keeping magnets away from computers). Some warnings are used to prevent something that may ruin the actual experiment.

PROJECT 1 THE FORCES AROUND YOU

IN THIS CHAPTER, YOU LEARN ABOUT FORCES. You play with magnets, move stuff with static electricity, swing water over your head while staying dry, and defy gravity with a string of beads.

WHAT IS A FORCE?

The experiments in this chapter all have something in common: they all explore forces.

So what is a force? The definition of a *force* is simple; it is a push or a pull on an object. If you have an object in front of you, push it across the table. You just applied a force to an object. Now pull it back toward you. Another force!

Every force has a direction. To show this direction, scientists draw arrows. If you push an object away from you (like a chair), the direction of that force is away from you. If you pull the object toward you, the direction of the force is toward you.

PUSH PULL

THE ARROWS SHOW THE DIRECTION OF THE FORCE

Forces can be big or small. If you push on something lightly, it is a small force. If you push harder, that force is bigger.

Forces can make things move, or make things move faster, or make moving things stop or change direction. Imagine hitting a baseball that has been pitched to you. The forces from your arms and the bat cause the ball flying through the air to change direction and to go at a different speed. Sometimes you can apply a force to something that is not moving and the object will . . . continue not to move! Imagine pushing against a wall; you are applying a force to the wall, but unless you are the Hulk the wall will remain motionless.

You may think that if something isn't moving that no forces are acting on it, but this is not true. Forces are all around you, and forces are always, at every moment, acting upon you! The biggest example of this is that everything on earth is being pulled down at all times by the force of gravity.

GRAVITY IS PULLING DOWN ON EVERYTHING.

You can't see gravity, but it is still a force. Gravity acts at a distance, and you could even consider gravity an *invisible* force. Other invisible forces include magnetic and electrical forces. For electrical forces, think of plugging in a fan. You can plug it in and turn it on, and electricity provides the force needed to move the fan blades.

One last rule that's good to know is that a moving object will continue to move in the same direction, and at the same speed, until another force acts on it. This is called *inertia*. At first, this rule may not seem to make sense because if you throw a ball, it will not stay in the air forever. But don't forget that the force of gravity is acting on the ball, pulling it down. Even the air itself acts as a force that slows the ball down!

This chapter contains activities on forces created by magnets, electricity, and more. I hope you have a blast experimenting.

MAKE A PAPER CLIP JUMP

Explore the invisible magnetic force in this fun and easy experiment.

Supplies

Magnetic wand (or relatively strong fridge magnet) | Paper clips (standard size)

MAKE A PAPER CLIP JUMP

Instructions

1 **Place your paper clip on the paper clip spot in the preceding figure.**

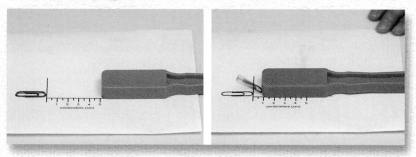

Sam Poon

2 **Take your magnetic wand and line it up with the 5 cm spot so that your wand is 5 cm away from the paper clip.**

3 **Move the magnetic wand slowly toward the paper clip.**

As you get closer, does the paper clip jump through the air toward your wand? How close is it?

The science

How cool is it that you can move an object without touching it? In this experiment, you moved the paper clip using a magnetic force. Magnets create an invisible magnetic field that pushes or pulls certain (magnetic) objects, even when the magnet isn't touching the object. Scientists draw magnetic fields using lines (curved and straight) and arrows, as shown in the figure.

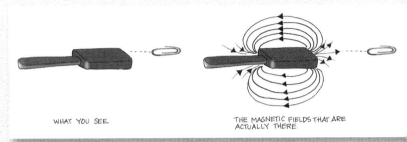

WHAT YOU SEE.

THE MAGNETIC FIELDS THAT ARE ACTUALLY THERE.

In your experiment, your magnet pulled your paper clip. Even though you couldn't see the force from your magnet, it was strong enough to make the paper clip jump through the air.

Going further

A *material* is what something is made out of. Not all materials can be pushed or pulled by your magnet. Explore items in your house to see what items are affected by the magnetic force. Try testing coins, bobby pins, thumbtacks, aluminum foil, and screws.

MAKE A PAPER CLIP REACH FOR THE SKY

Demonstrate the power of magnetic force by suspending a paper clip in the air!

Supplies

Magnetic wand	Scissors
Paper clip	Duct tape
Thread	Table, ledge, or a pile of books
Piece of cardboard	at least a foot high

Instructions

Overview: You are going to tie a paper clip to a piece of thread and anchor that paper clip and thread to the ground using a piece of cardboard. You will then suspend the paper clip with your magnet.

1 **Tape your magnetic wand to your ledge or book pile using duct tape, as shown in the figure.**

Duct tape can ruin surfaces, so please check with an adult before taping directly to the furniture.

Sam Poon

2 **Cut your piece of cardboard so that you have about 1 foot on each side.**

3 **Use scissors to make a small hole in the center of the cardboard.**

4 **Cut a long piece of thread.**

The thread should be about a foot longer than the distance from the floor (or table) to your magnetic wand.

5 **Tie one end of the thread to your paperclip.**

6 **Thread the other end of your string through the cardboard piece, using the figure as a reference.**

I pulled the end of the thread out from under the cardboard and taped it (temporarily) to the cardboard.

7 **Place the center of the cardboard, with the thread and paper clip facing up, on the floor directly below your magnet.**

8 **Pick up your paper clip (tied to the string) and hover it about an inch below the magnetic wand.**

You should feel the magnetic force pulling on the paper clip.

Sam Poon

9 **Adjust the length of the string so that the paper clip remains about 1 inch or less below the magnet (without you touching it), as shown in the figure.**

10 **Tape the bottom piece of string to the cardboard.**

Now your paper clip is being held in the air by magnetic force! The magnetic force is pulling up on your paper clip. What forces are pulling down on the paper clip to prevent it from touching the magnet?

The science

In this experiment, you used magnetic force to suspend your paper clip in the air. Normally, objects fall to the ground because the force of gravity pulls them down. But here, when your paper clip was close enough to the magnet, the magnetic force was greater than the force of gravity. (The closer you get to the magnet, the magnetic field — and therefore the magnetic force — becomes stronger.) For me, the magnetic field was strong enough to hold the paper clip in the air when the paper clip was about an inch away. Did you have the same results?

Going further

Can you find other magnetic materials that you can tie to the string and hold in the air with your magnet? If you have two magnetic wands, what happens when you put them side by side or on top of each other? Does anything change?

STATIC ELECTRICITY: MAKE A PLASTIC BAG STICKY

Static electricity can create a force, and, like the forces that come from magnets and gravity, this force is invisible. Find out how to create static electricity in this simple experiment.

Note: This experiment works best when it's dry outside. If it's raining or humid, it will not work as well.

Supplies

Thin plastic produce bag from supermarket

Fabric item that contains wool or nylon

Plastic comb

Scissors

A flat surface

Sam Poon

Instructions

1 Cut off a rectangular piece of the plastic produce bag.

My piece is about 2 inches x 6 inches

2 Place your plastic on the table and make your observations.

What do you see and notice? Is the bag sticking to the table?

3 Rub the plastic several times with your cloth, as shown in the figure, and make more observations.

4 **Turn the plastic over and rub the other side several times.**

5 **Pinch the corner of the plastic and peel it off the table.**

What happens?

6 **Crinkle your plastic into a ball and rub it against the smooth side of your plastic comb.**

7 **Unfold the plastic and place it on the table.**

Is it sticking now?

The science

Everything around you, and even your own body, contains these tiny pieces called electrons. Electrons are really, really small and when they move around, they make electricity. When something has extra electrons, it has static electricity.

Some materials hold on tight to their electrons and don't like to share them, but other materials are like, "We have extra electrons! Come on and take them!"

Fabrics like wool or nylon give away their electrons really easily. When you rub the fabric on the plastic, it gives the plastic extra electrons. These extra electrons pull the plastic to the table. (**Note:** With extra electrons, the plastic will stick to some things, like your clothes and the table, but not to everything.)

Finally, when you rub the plastic onto the comb, the extra electrons move off your plastic and onto the comb so that your plastic is no longer as sticky.

Going further

Try rubbing different materials on your bag to create static electricity.

BEND A STREAM OF WATER

In this experiment, you harness static electricity by bending a stream of water. This experiment works best when it's dry outside. If it's raining or humid, it will not work as well.

Supplies

Plastic water bottle with lid	Wool or nylon fabric
Thumbtack	Large bowl or go outside
Balloon or plastic comb	Another person (optional)

Instructions

1. **Blow up your balloon (or use a comb).**

2. **Fill your plastic bottle with water and screw the cap on firmly.**

3. **Use your thumbtack to make a hole about halfway down the side of the bottle.**

4. **Rub your balloon many times over with your fabric.**

   Try to rub over a large area of the balloon. Keep your balloon in your hand.

5. **If another person is there, have her hold the bottle in the air, with the hole facing down.**

Make sure that the bottle is over the bowl to catch the water or go outside.

6. **Gently squeeze the bottle to create a thin stream of water, as shown in the figure.**

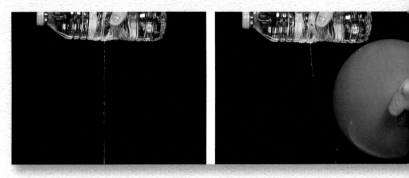

Sam Poo▸

This next step requires a steady hand.

1 **Place your balloon about 2 inches away from the water stream and then slowly move it closer and closer to the stream without actually touching the water.**

If your balloon accidently gets wet, dry it off really well with paper towels, but do not dry it with the fabric you are using to charge it.

Do you see the water stream bending?

The science

Electrons on the balloon interacting with the water stream cause the water stream to bend. (If you're not sure what electrons are, try the experiment before this one.) When you rub the balloon (or a comb) with your fabric, the extra electrons on the wool or nylon get rubbed off onto the balloon.

Electrons are charged. Charges are a very important part of electricity. In fact, electricity is basically charges, like electrons, moving around. Think about how you say you're going to charge your phone battery. That just means electrons are moving around in a certain way.

Scientists say electrons have a negative charge (-). It turns out these negatively charged electrons don't "like" other electrons. Electrons move away from electrons and move toward things that are positively charged. In this case, opposites really do attract!

The negative charge on your balloon or comb attracts positive charges in the water, causing the stream to bend toward your charged object.

Where are the positive charges in the water coming from? Good question! Water molecules have a side with a weak positive charge and another side with a weak negative charge. It is commonly said that, in this experiment, the negatively charged item is attracting the positively charged side of the water molecules. But this may not be true!

It has been convincingly argued that in fact impurities in the water are charged, and these charged impurities are being attracted to the comb. The scientific knowledge base is always evolving and expanding!

BEND A STREAM OF WATER

Go further
Try bending water with different charged materials. If your material gets wet, will it still bend the water? How thick of a stream can you bend?

LAUGH AT THE FORCE OF GRAVITY

This amazing demonstration requires a long string of beads, but the effect is worth the extra purchase!

Supplies

String of beads (about 50 feet) | Rubber band, duct tape, or permanent marker

A large cup or 500 mL beaker

Note: I used a 50 foot string of 6 mm diameter (faux) pearls ordered off Amazon for under $4. Another option is to glue together multiple Mardi Gras necklaces. (Cut each necklace and string them together using a glue gun.) These necklaces are usually 2.5 feet long when cut, and you need at least 10 necklaces, but 20 is better! You can find them online, at party stores, or at dollar stores.

Instructions

1 **Find the free end of your beads and wrap the tape or rubber band around it.**

Alternatively, you can color it with a permanent marker. You just want to make sure that you can easily find the end later.

2 **Unravel your string of beads (or make it easy to unravel).**

 Careful not to knot the beads!

3 **Mark the other free end with the rubber band, tape, or permanent marker.**

You are going to put your beads in your cup using a special technique. You cannot just dump them in the cup.

4 **Place one free end of the beads into the cup.**

5 **Now slowly feed the beads into the cup as in the figure.**

The trick is to make sure that the beads you put in most recently are always on top of the old beads.

6 **When your beads are loaded, stand up and hold the cup in the air, give the free end a gentle tug, and drop it to the floor.**

Watch the path the beads take as they exit the cup.

Sam Poon

The science

Did you see your beads lift into the air as they left the cup? The forces that cause this to happen are pretty complicated! Scientists found that each little bead behaves like a tiny rod (even though they're round). As a bead gets pulled in the air, the bottom of the bead hits the beads below it, which provides a force that makes the beads jump up in the air.

Until very recently, scientists didn't even know how this gravity-defying effect even happened. To figure out which forces were causing this effect, scientists called physicists used expensive cameras to watch the beads fall in slow motion. They then used math to figure out what was happening. If you study science, this is the cool stuff you get to do.

Going further

This effect was originally discovered with metal ball chains, which are a little expensive but are available from Amazon. Will this effect work with plain string or a shorter strand of beads?

SWING, SWING: CUP IS UPSIDE DOWN, BUT THE WATER WON'T FALL DOWN

In this experiment, you swing containers filled with water upside down and over your head. Do you think you can stay dry?

Supplies

1- or 2-liter soda bottle	Water
String	An outdoor space
Scissors	Single-hole punch or thumbtack (optional)

Instructions

1 Cut off the bottom one-third of your soda bottle.

2 Make four evenly spaced small holes near the top of your cut bottle (see figure).

Alternatively, you can use a thumbtack to start the holes and then use scissors to make the holes bigger.

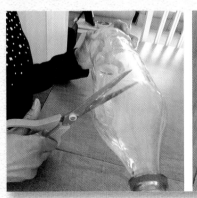
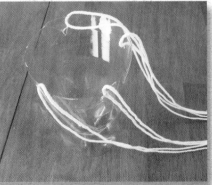

3 **Cut four pieces of string the same length.**

For a 1-liter bottle, I cut each string a little over 3 feet. For a 2-liter bottle, I cut them closer to 4 feet.

4 **Thread one piece of string through a hole and then tie the two free ends of the string in a knot.**

5 **Repeat for the other three holes.**

6 **Tie your strings from the four holes in one big knot.**

Your apparatus is complete and ready to test.

7 **Fill the container about halfway full with water and find a space outdoors.**

8 **Holding onto the knot in your strings, swing the container in the air somewhat quickly (see figure).**

What happened to the water?

The science

You should have found that you could swing the bottle around without the water falling out! How did this happen?

Gravity is a relatively weak force. To make anything go up and not fall, you simply have to have a force that is stronger than gravity pulling or pushing it up.

If there are no forces on a moving object, the object will continue to move straight ahead. In this experiment, you used your strings to spin the container around in a circle. This action puts a *centripetal force* on the water and the container, which pulls the water toward your hand. The force of gravity is pulling the water down. If you are swinging your rope fast enough, the centripetal force is greater than gravity. Centripetal force and inertia are enough to prevent gravity from making the water fall all over your head!

CENTRIPETAL FORCE
GRAVITY
INERTIA

Note: Although represented by an arrow in the figure, inertia itself is not a force.

Think about it: Gravity is also acting on the container, yet the container doesn't fall down during this activity either. The same forces acting on the container are acting on the water.

Going further

Using different size containers, hold your strings at different lengths and spin your rope at different speeds. Just make sure that you do this outside! What do you discover?

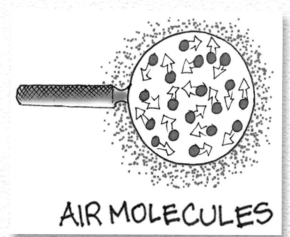

AIR MOLECULES

YOU ARE ABOUT TO CONDUCT SOME REALLY COOL EXPERIMENTS THAT WILL HELP YOU UNDERSTAND AIR, AIR PRESSURE, WIND, AND WEATHER. It's funny; air is around people all the time, but because they can't see it, it can be hard to understand what air actually is.

It turns out that when you start to study air and air pressure, you can see some really unexpected and crazy things! Understanding air help you understand the weather patterns you see around you. The experiments in this chapter help you gain a whole new appreciation of air and weather.

AIR, AIR IS EVERYWHERE

Air is a gas. Like all gases, air is made up of little tiny pieces of stuff called *molecules* (specifically, nitrogen and oxygen molecules). Molecules are so small and tiny that you can't see them. They are so light that they can float.

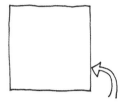

WHAT AIR LOOKS LIKE TO US (NOTHING).

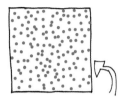

WHAT AIR IS: TINY PIECES OF STUFF (MOLECULES).

It's important to understand that molecules are something physical and real. Imagine that you had an entire room full of floating bouncy balls, and then the balls shrunk and shrunk, until eventually you couldn't see them. That is what air is like.

You can see that air takes up space when you blow up a balloon or pump up a tire. When you blow into a balloon, you are literally putting more molecules inside the balloon. These air molecules push against the balloon and make it bigger.

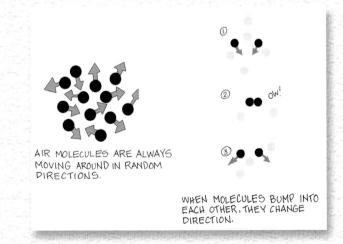

AIR MOLECULES ARE ALWAYS MOVING AROUND IN RANDOM DIRECTIONS.

WHEN MOLECULES BUMP INTO EACH OTHER, THEY CHANGE DIRECTION.

An interesting thing about molecules is that they're always moving, especially the molecules in gases. Because the molecules are moving around, they bump into each other a lot, which makes them change direction. Think of a bunch of bumper cars, hitting each other and changing directions. That's similar to what happens with air molecules.

A DEFLATED BALLOON WILL HAVE THE SAME CONCENTRATION OF AIR AS THE AIR OUTSIDE THE BALLOON.

A BLOWN-UP BALLOON HAS MORE AIR (IN A GIVEN SPACE) THAN THE AIR OUTSIDE OF IT. THE AIR PRESSURE INSIDE THE BALLOON IS HIGHER.

Because air molecules are physical, moving objects, when they bump into another object, like a wall or your body, they apply a force to the object. (You can read about forces in Chapter 1). When a lot of air molecules are in a particular space (and/or they're moving really fast), scientists say that the air pressure is high. *Air pressure* is the pressure exerted by the weight of air on an object. When there is less air and/or the air molecules are moving slowly, the air pressure is said to be low. In the balloon example, the air pressure inside blown-up is much higher than the air pressure outside of it.

Air moves from areas of *high pressure* to areas of *low pressure*. This fact explains why air rushes out of a balloon when you open up the balloon mouth as opposed to rushing into it. You can think of the air inside the inflated balloon as crowded, and when the air has a chance to escape this crowded environment, it does.

Enjoy experimenting with wind, weather, and the weird tricks you can do with air pressure.

BALLOON ROCKET

Use changes in air pressure to make a balloon rocket across the room.

Supplies

String (several feet)

Balloon

Straw

Clear tape

A twist tie or a friend to help

Instructions

1 **Cut your straw so that it's 4 to 5 inches long.**

2 **Find a place where you can tie a piece of string across the room.**

I went outside and used a support beam and a tree. You can also use chairs, door knobs, or anywhere else you can tie a string.

3 **Thread your string through your straw.**

4 **Tie each end of the string to the spots you found in Step 2, as shown in the figure.**

The string should be tight but not too tight.

5 **Bring the straw to one end of the string (the higher end if the ends are not even).**

6 **Blow up your balloon but don't tie it closed.**

Sam Poon

1 **Either wrap a twist tie around the end of your balloon so that no air escapes or have a friend hold the mouth of the balloon closed.**

Use two pieces of tape to attach the balloon to the straw, as shown in the figure. Don't let air escape.

Make sure the mouth of the balloon is facing away from the rest of the string, as shown in the figure.

8 **To unwrap the twist tie, pinch the neck of the balloon with one hand while you unwrap the tie.**

This will prevent the air from escaping until you are ready. If your friend is holding the balloon, tell him to get ready.

9 **Let go of the balloon and watch it fly across the room.**

The science

Did you see your balloon fly across the room on your string? The air pressure inside your balloon was higher than the air pressure outside the balloon. When you let go of the balloon, air quickly moved from a high pressure area to a low pressure area. As the air escaped, it provided a force that propelled the balloon forward.

If you would like to know more about air pressure, read the "Air, Air Is Everywhere" section earlier in this chapter.

Sam Poon

Going further

How far can you make the balloon travel? Does the straw length affect the rocket? Does the rocket work better when the string slopes downward rather than straight across?

THE IMPOSSIBLE TASK: BLOWING A BALL INTO A BOTTLE

The task in this experiment sounds easy, but the science of air pressure makes it impossible!

Supplies

2 identical plastic bottles

Scissors

Small piece of aluminum foil or paper

Instructions

1 Cut out a small piece of paper or aluminum foil.

I used a piece that was 4 x 5 inches.

2 Crinkle the paper or foil into a ball.

You want the ball to be smaller than the opening of a plastic soda bottle but not too much smaller. Use the figure as a guide.

3 Place the soda bottle on its side and then place the ball in the mouth of the bottle.

Sam Poor

4 Try to blow the ball into the bottle.

Did the ball go in? If so, make another ball that is a little bigger.

5 Repeat Step 4 until you find that no matter how much you try, the ball won't go in the bottle.

6 Take your second bottle and confirm that you can't blow the ball into it either.

7 **Cut a hole in the bottom of the second bottle, as shown in the figure.**

8 **Try to blow the ball into the bottle again.**

What happened?

9 **If you still cannot blow the ball into the bottle, cut a larger hole and try again.**

Sam Poon

The science

How can it be that, at a certain size, the ball becomes impossible to blow into the bottle? The answer is that the bottle might look empty, but it's actually full of air. When you try to blow the ball in, you're also blowing extra air into the bottle. The air you're blowing in pushes other air out.

Another important thing is that when you blow air, it makes a low pressure stream. The low pressure in front of the ball, combined with air leaving the bottle, pushes out the ball.

When you make a hole in the back of the bottle, the air now has room to escape without pushing out the ball, so now you can blow the ball into the bottle!

Going further

Try this experiment with other materials, such as a toilet paper roll. Cover one opening with a piece of duct tape or paper, put a large ball of paper in the other opening, and blow. Can you think of other ways to do something similar?

FOUNTAIN AIR PRESSURE TRICK

Air pressure can behave in some strange ways. This experiment shows you how air pressure provides a very real force.

Supplies

Plastic water bottle with cap	Water
Thumbtack	Wide dish to catch water (or do experiment outside)

Instructions

1 **Fill the plastic bottle up to the top with water.**

2 **Screw the lid on the bottle tightly.**

3 **Put the bottle in your wide dish to catch the water (or go outside).**

4 **Stick your thumbtack into your bottle about halfway down the bottle to make a hole, as shown in the figure.**

Sam Poo

You may need to cut off the bottle's label. Try to squeeze the bottle as little as possible.

5 **Remove the thumbtack.**

6 **Let go of the bottle and stand back.**

Is the water squirting out?

7 **Squeeze the water bottle, gently at first, to confirm your hole is there.**

8 **Without squeezing the bottle too much (try holding it at the neck), unscrew the cap and let go.**

What happens?

9 **Again, without squeezing the bottle much, replace the cap.**

What happens?

Sam Poon

10 **If your fountain starts to drip instead of squirt, try refilling the water bottle.**

Adding water to the bottle will add pressure inside the bottle, which makes it squirt out more.

The science

Air pressure is constantly pushing on everything, including your bottle. With the cap screwed on, the pressure inside the bottle was not enough to overcome the air pressure outside the bottle. (Surface tension plays a role here, too.) Therefore, the water did not squirt out. When you opened the cap, suddenly air pressure pushed down on the water in the bottle, creating enough additional pressure to push the water out of the hole.

Going further

Explore the effects of water pressure. Make additional holes in other areas of your bottle. How does it affect your experiment? Do you see a difference when the holes are higher or lower in the bottle?

JUST ONE BREATH: MAKE A WINDBAG AND BLOW IT UP QUICK

You can change the air pressure in front of you just by blowing air from your mouth. You can use this ability to do cool tricks, like blowing up a large bag in a single breath. In this experiment, you learn how to make and quickly blow up a windbag.

Supplies

Trash bag (kitchen size is fine) | Duct tape
| Scissors

Part I: Making the windbag

Overview: In Part I, you cut two strips off your garbage bag and tape them together to make one long bag.

1 **If your garbage bag has an uneven top, cut it so that the top is straight.**

2 **Cut a strip off either side of the garbage bag, a little smaller than half of the size of the bag, as shown in the figure.**

You are going to cut from the top to the bottom of the bag on both sides.

3 **Cut off a piece of duct tape that is as long as your new strips and use it to seal the open side of one of the strips you just cut.**

In other words, tape up the side of one of the strips so that it's a long but skinny bag.

4 **Repeat Step 3 for the second strip.**

Tape the sides.

Cut out your strips.

Cut the bottom off one strip.

5 **Cut off the bottom of only one of the strips so that it's open at both ends like a tunnel.**

⚠ WARNING

Make sure you cut the bottom of only one strip, not both. I call this strip Strip A.

6 **Put the open top of the second strip (Strip B) around one of the open ends of Strip A.**

🎯 TIP

Check the figure in Part II of this experiment for guidance.

7 **Seal the two strips together with duct tape.**

You should now have a long and skinny bag, with all sides but the top sealed together. This is your windbag.

Part II: Blowing up the bag

1 Place your windbag from Part I flat on a table.

2 Try cupping the bag around your mouth to blow it up, as shown in the figure (labeled Technique 1).

Did it work? Now try another way.

3 Make your head level with the bag so that you'll be blowing straight into the bag.

You may need to crouch down.

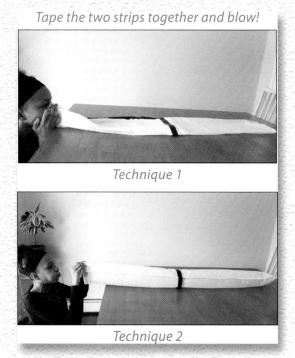

Tape the two strips together and blow!

Technique 1

Technique 2

4 Keep your head about 1 foot away from the bag and open the top so that you can blow into it.

5 Make your mouth into an O shape, take a deep breath, and blow (Technique 2 in the figure).

6 Use your hand to seal off the end of the bag and then push your hand up to trap the air at one end of the bag.

Did you blow up the bag?

The science

When you blow a stream of air from your mouth, the air in that stream is low pressure. Air flows from high to low pressure. High pressure air surrounding the stream will actually be pulled into your low pressure air stream and follow the air into a bag. So the air filling up the bag is not just coming from your lungs but being pulled in from the outside air.

Sometimes you can feel this effect when a car goes by and creates a stream of low pressure air just like you did with your breath.

Going further

What happens when you make your bag skinnier, fatter, shorter, or longer? How long of a bag can you blow up in one breath?

MAKE WATER FLOAT, MAKE WATER SINK

Air has a temperature. If you've ever seen smoke rising, you may realize that hot air goes up, and cold air goes down! It can be hard to demonstrate this effect with air itself, but it turns out water behaves in a similar way.

In this experiment, you explore the effects of mixing warm and cold water. As you watch the results, keep in mind that mixing warm and cold air does mostly the same thing!

Supplies

Two clear plastic cups	Very warm water
Two small dishes	Cold water
Plastic spoon	Ice
Duct tape	Permanent marker
Blue and red food dye	

Instructions

Overview: You are going to add dyed warm water to a cup of cold water and dyed cold water to a cup of warm water.

1 **With your permanent marker, label one cup Cold Water and the other cup Warm Water; set the warm water cup aside.**

2 **Fill the cold water cup and one small dish with cold water and ice cubes.**

3 **Fill the other cup and small dish with very warm water from the faucet.**

The water should be warm but not painful to the touch.

4 Put a few drops of blue food coloring in the small dish (but not in the cup) with cold water and set both aside as the water gets ice cold.

5 Put a few drops of red food coloring in the small dish with warm water (but not in the cup).

You're going to make a mini-ladle using your plastic spoon – take a look at the one I made in the following figure.

Sam Poon

6 If you're using a plastic spoon that bends without breaking, bend it and reinforce the bend with strips of duct tape.

If the spoon doesn't bend, have an adult break the spoon off from the handle. Then reattach the handle using duct tape so that it looks like the figure.

7 Remove any ice left in your Cold Water cup.

Make sure the water is ice cold.

8 Using your ladle, take some blue, cold water from the small bowl and slowly and gently lower the ladle into the warm water cup; slowly and gently remove the spoon.

9 Repeat Step 8 several times.

10 Look at the cup from the side, not just the top.

What happens to the blue water?

11 Use your ladle to repeat Steps 8 and 9, but this time put the warm, red water into the cold water cup.

12 Look at the cup from the side, not just down from the top.

What happened this time? Is it different than what happened with the blue water?

Sam Poo

The science

You should have found that the blue cold water sank to the bottom of the warm water cup, (which caused all the water to turn blue). In contrast, you should have found that the warm red water stayed on the top of your cold water cup. Why? It is because, like air, hot water rises, and cold water sinks. So your blue, cold water sank, and your warm, red water floated!

So, why exactly does the warmer water rise, and colder water sink? Cold water is denser than hot water, which means that the cold water is heavier than the warm water for a given volume. The same thing is true for hot and cold air.

These facts (that hot air and water rise, and cold air and water sink) are responsible for lots of weather! In air, when hot and cold air meet each other, they move around a lot because the hot air starts to go up, and the cold air down. This movement creates wind. In water, hot and cold water meeting creates currents.

Going further

Try putting cold blue water in the cold water cup and warm red water in the warm water cup. What happened? What would happen if you put an ice cube in warm or cold water?

PROJECT 3 SOUND WAVES

Sam Poon

SOUND HELPS YOU COMMUNICATE AND NAVIGATE THE WORLD, BUT WHAT IS SOUND, EXACTLY? In this chapter, you explore the fun properties of sound waves and make some cool noises in the process.

WHAT IS SOUND?

Tap your finger against a table or wall or snap your fingers. Do you hear the sound? Think for a second. What is a *sound,* and how are you able to hear it?

Think of a speaker playing music. For you to hear the music, the sound must travel from the speaker to your ears. And what is between the speaker and your ear? Air! That means the sound must travel through the air. So one important point about sound is that sound waves travel through the air.

A *sound wave* is a vibration. *Vibrations* are what occur when something moves very fast and repeatedly. (Think of your phone on vibrate mode.)

Sometimes you can feel the vibrations that create sound. For example, if you gently place your fingers on your throat (as in the figure) and make a loud "ahhhhh" sound or start talking, you will notice that your throat vibrates. These vibrations create the sound waves.

How do these sound waves or vibrations travel through the air? Air is made up of molecules, which are physical, real things that can be moved around. The vibrations that come from speakers, snapping, or knocking on a door actually vibrate the molecules in the air. The vibrations travel through the air and into your ear. Inside your ear, the vibrations in the air vibrate your eardrum, which eventually sends a signal to your brain that you heard a sound.

In this chapter, you explore these sound waves and vibrations. Have fun!

WHO KNEW YOU COULD DO THAT WITH A BALLOON?

I love experiments that help you discover the unexpected. In this experiment, create unusual vibrations (meaning sounds) by spinning a hex nut inside a balloon!

Supplies

Hex nut

Balloon

Twist tie (optional)

Instructions

1 **Place a hex nut into your balloon.**

Make sure the hex nut has fallen into the main chamber of the balloon and is not stuck in the balloon mouth.

2 **Blow up the balloon.**

 Please be very careful to not accidently inhale and swallow the hex nut.

3 **Tie the balloon closed.**

If you want to be able to open the balloon easily as you experiment, use a twist tie instead of knotting it.

4 **Take the balloon in both your hands and make circular movements with your hands.**

Make a similar movement to the one you would make if you were holding a pot of water and swishing the water around.

The hex nut should start circling around inside the balloon. Do you hear the noise it makes? If you make the hex nut travel faster or slower, what happens? Pay attention to your hands and see whether you can feel the wall of the balloon vibrating.

The science

The way in which the hex nut and balloon come in contact make a particular set of vibrations that create this unique sound. When the hex nut is moving faster, the vibrations increase in frequency and become higher pitched.

Going further

Try multiple hex nuts or other objects in the balloons. Blow up the balloons to different sizes. Does it make a difference? Do different-sized hex nuts make different sounds?

RUBBER BAND MUSIC

Use rubber bands to explore sounds and create an item similar to a guitar.

Supplies

Rubber bands, various sizes

Small dish(es) or plastic bowl(s)

Duct tape

Safety glasses

Instructions

1 **Pick several rubber bands of different widths that are big enough to wrap around your dish.**

2 **With your safety glasses on, wrap your rubber bands around your dish.**

You want the string to be fairly tight, but not so tight that it will break. If your rubber bands are too long for your dish, you can tie a knot in your bands as I did for one of mine (see yellow rubber band in figure).

 Rubber bands can go flying and injure your eyes or other body parts. Please wear eye protection and be careful not to let your bands snap off your dish.

3 **Cut a piece of duct tape and place it over the side of your dish and rubber bands, as shown in the figure, to secure your bands in place.**

Use your fingertip or fingernail to push down the tape so that all parts of the tape are in direct contact with the rubber band.

4 **Repeat Step 3 for the other side of your dish.**

Your rubber band instrument is now complete.

5 Pluck the bands and pay attention to the sounds.

Do bands of different widths make different noises? Does the sound change if a band is stretched tighter or looser?

The science

When you snap your rubber band, the band vibrates, sending vibrations through the air, which your brain hears as sound. The vibrations, and therefore the sounds, will be different based on many factors, such as the size and length of the rubber band as well as how tightly it is pulled. The shape and size of the dish will also affect the sounds you hear.

Everything else being equal, thicker bands will vibrate more slowly than thinner bands, which results in lower sounds. In contrast, thinner bands will make higher pitched sounds when plucked. The tighter you stretch a band, the higher the sound. Finally, shorter strings will also produce higher pitched sounds than longer strings.

Going further

Test different containers and make each rubber band a different tightness. Do you hear different sounds?

SOUND MOVES THROUGH A STRING

Sound waves, or vibrations, often travel through the air, but sound can move through materials, too. Here, you will create a sound that travels through a string.

Supplies

Cotton twine

Metal spoon

Scissors

Pencil or pen

Instructions

1 Cut a piece of string about 1.5 feet long.

2 Tie one end of the string around the spoon, as shown in the figure.

3 Wrap the string around your index finger two to three times and let the spoon hang freely.

4 Pick up your pencil or pen in your other hand and gently tap the spoon.

Can you feel the vibrations that traveled up the string?

5 Stick your wrapped index finger in one ear.

6 Bend at the waist so that the spoon is hanging from the string freely and touching nothing.

7 Use your pen or pencil to tap the spoon one time.

What do you hear? How long does the sound last?

8 Tap the spoon again and then grab it with your free hand.

What happens?

The science

Sound waves normally reach your ears through the air, but in this experiment, the sound waves, or the vibrations, traveled through the string and into your ear! (When I say "traveled through the string," I mean the string was literally vibrating.) These vibrations eventually vibrate your eardrum, allowing you to hear the sound. Sound waves can travel through lots of materials, like string, windows, or walls.

Going further

Tie other objects to your string and see what they sound like. One popular item to try is a coat hanger. Tie string to metal and plastic coat hangers and compare the sounds!

MAKE SALT JUMP WITH YOUR VOICE

In this fun experiment, you create vibrations with your voice and make salt bounce.

Supplies

Condiment cup

Balloon

Scissors

Rubber band (not too thick)

Salt

A strong voice

Bowl

Plastic wrap

Instructions

1 **Stick your scissors in the neck of the balloon and cut up along one side, as shown in the figure.**

Sam Poon

2 Stretch the balloon over the opening of the condiment cup, as shown in the figure.

3 Wrap the rubber band around the balloon and cup so that the balloon membrane is fairly tight.

4 Place your cup and balloon into your bowl (to prevent a mess).

5 Sprinkle a thin layer of salt onto your balloon membrane

6 Practice a deep but loud yell two to three times.

The yell you need is strong but not high pitched. Maybe think of an extreme burp or the sound a movie monster or dinosaur would make.

7 Cup your hand around your mouth, aim at the balloon membrane and then make a deep, loud yell.

8 If you do not see the salt bouncing, yell louder.

What do you see?

9 To confirm you are not simply blowing the salt with air, put plastic wrap on top of the bowl and yell again.

The science

In this activity, you are literally making something move using only your voice. When you yell, your throat or vocal cords vibrate, and those vibrations vibrate the air. The vibrations in the air travel and hit the balloon membrane, making it vibrate as well. When the balloon membrane vibrates, the salt bounces.

The plastic wrap doesn't block the sound because sound can travel through many materials. Think about how hard it is to make a room soundproof.

Going further

What other materials can you make vibrate? Rice? Quinoa? What happens if your yell becomes high pitched? Quieter? Louder?

ROJECT 4 CHEMISTRY

Sam Poon

WHEN PEOPLE THINK OF SCIENCE, THEY OFTEN THINK OF CHEMISTRY BECAUSE THEY ASSOCIATE SCIENCE WITH BUBBLING POTIONS AND BIG EXPLOSIONS. In this chapter, you make some fizzing potions, do some surprising science tricks, and explore the properties of different materials!

WHAT IS CHEMISTRY?

Chemistry is the study of the materials that things are made of and how those materials interact with each other. Chemists are interested in molecules. Molecules are way too small for you to see. (If you made a line of molecules across your hand, you would be able to fit around 100,000,000 molecules.)

Chemists explore the properties of materials, like how hard or elastic they are or how much water a material can absorb. They also study chemical reactions. A *chemical reaction* is a process that takes one or more materials and makes brand new materials. For example, oxygen in the air will react with metals on a nail to create rust. Wood burning in air is also a chemical reaction, one that releases a lot of gas and heat.

RUST COMES FROM A CHEMICAL REACTION!

Not just any change in a material is a chemical reaction. For example, ice melting is a chemical process but not a chemical reaction. (It's a change in the state of water from frozen to liquid water.) I hope the experiments in this chapter help you learn lots about Chemistry!

TIE-DYE MILK

This fun and pretty experiment teaches you about the properties of milk, food dye, and dish soap!

Supplies

Whole milk

Food coloring, two or more colors (water based, not gel based)

Two cotton swabs, such as a Q-tip

Bowl (smaller is better to not waste milk)

Instructions

1 **Fill your bowl with milk.**

2 **Put several drops of food coloring into your bowl.**

3 **Gently place one cotton swab in the center of the bowl.**

   What happens?

4 **Put a little dish soap on your second cotton swab.**

5 **Put your soapy cotton swab into the center of the bowl.**

   What happens?

6 **Continue to place your cotton swab in the bowl in different spots until it stops having an effect.**

Sam Poon

The science

To understand this experiment, you first need to understand that dish soap is made specifically to break up things like fats and proteins in order to help you get grease and food off of your dishes. And milk (especially whole milk) has fats and proteins.

You also need to know about surface tension. *Surface tension* is a property that comes from water molecules binding tightly together at the surface of a liquid. This property causes certain items to float on top of a liquid or water to form small droplets when sitting on certain surfaces.

When you add the dish soap to the milk, the soap reduces the surface tension and spreads across the surface, spreading out the dye. The soap also binds to the fats and proteins in the milk, which causes additional movement in the dish.

The food dye itself does not contribute to the effect of mixing the soap and milk, but it's there so that you can see what is happening.

Going further

Test how important fat is to this experiment by repeating the experiment using lower fat milks (2%, 1%, or skim). You can also try it in water (which, of course, has no fat) by floating very small pieces of aluminum foil on the water surface and seeing whether they move when you add the soap.

EVERY SCIENTIST NEEDS A LITTLE OOBLECK

In school, you're taught how to classify objects as solid, liquid, or gas, but it turns out not everything can be so simply defined. Some materials can't make up their minds; sometimes they act like liquids, and sometimes they acts like solids.

In this experiment, you'll make an *oobleck* (the name is from a Dr. Seuss book) with cornstarch and water to see one of these sometimes-solid, sometimes-liquid materials in action.

Supplies

Cornstarch	Water
Bowl	Newspaper or other material to cover table and floor

Instructions

1 **Put ½ cup of water into your bowl.**

2 **Measure out 1 cup of cornstarch and add part of it to your water; mix with your hands until the cornstarch dissolves.**

3 Continue to add cornstarch until you've added the entire cup.

As you add more and more cornstarch, the mixture starts to thicken.

If your mixture is still too runny, add a tablespoon or so more of cornstarch.

Your oobleck is complete. Now the fun starts.

4 Begin by playing around with the oobleck.

What observations can you make?

5 Try (carefully) punching the oobleck and then let your hand sink in.

Can you pull your hand out quickly, or do you have to move it slowly to get out of the oobleck?

The science

The cornstarch/water mixtures has the properties of both a solid and a liquid. Materials that have this property have a fancy name called *non-Newtonian fluids*. The factor that determines whether the oobleck will act as a solid or liquid is the amount of pressure or force you put on it. When you punch it, it acts like a solid because of the strong force. But when you slowly sink your hand into it, the force is low, and so it acts like a liquid!

There are lots of examples of non-Newtonian fluids around you, and even in you! Ketchup, shampoo, and blood are all examples. (Sometimes, though, these act in an opposite way from oobleck. Ketchup, for example, acts like a liquid under pressure and a solid otherwise.)

Going further

Make oobleck in a large enough container that you can walk on it. Try running fast or jumping and see how long it takes before you sink. Explore other non-Newtonian fluids around your home.

BOUNCE AN EGG

In this experiment, you explore an interesting chemical reaction that allows you to (gently) bounce a naked egg!

Supplies

Egg

Vinegar

Cup (clear is best)

Instructions

1 **Carefully put your egg in the cup.**

2 **Pour vinegar into the cup so that it covers the egg.**

Look closely at the egg. What do you see?

3 **Let the egg soak overnight.**

Feel free to check in on it occasionally and make observations.

4 **After about 24 hours, gently pick up the egg and rinse it off.**

5 **Gently rub the eggshell, as shown in the figure.**

What happens?

Sam Poon

6 Pour some fresh vinegar in your cup and put your egg back in the cup.

7 After another 24 hours, gently take your egg out and rinse it off.

8 If you gently drop the egg onto the table from a short distance (a few inches), you may find that your egg bounces!

The science

In this experiment, you created a chemical reaction by mixing the vinegar and the eggshell. This reaction dissolved the shell, but the egg was held in place by a thin membrane inside of the shell. The inside of the egg is more or less normal, as you can see in the figure, but the membrane won't crack like a shell, so you can gently bounce the egg.

The bubbles that you see forming on the surface of the egg are filled with a gas called carbon dioxide. Carbon dioxide was created by this reaction.

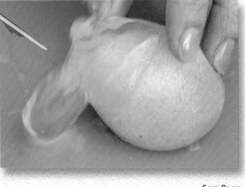

Sam Poon

Going further

Does vinegar travel inside the egg in this experiment? Add a few drops of food coloring to the vinegar and leave it overnight to see what happens.

BLOW UP A BALLOON WITH A CHEMICAL REACTION

It's fun to play around with chemical reactions. In this experiment, you blow up a balloon using a classic acid-base reaction.

Supplies

Plastic water bottle

Vinegar

Balloon

Spoon

Baking soda

Small piece of paper (about 2 x 2 inches)

Instructions

1 **Carefully pour about ¼ cup vinegar into your water bottle.**

2 **Put baking soda into your balloon.**

This step can be a little tricky. I suggest rolling your paper into a funnel of sorts, as shown in the figure. (Don't make either opening too small.) Put the bottom of your funnel into the balloon neck and put about two spoonfuls of baking soda into the balloon.

3 **Without dumping out the baking soda, place the mouth of the balloon over the neck of the water bottle.**

You are now ready for your experiment to begin.

4 **Dump the baking soda from the balloon into the vinegar.**

Make sure that you shake it all out. If baking soda is stuck in the neck of the balloon, the experiment won't work.

5 Observe your balloon and the reaction in the bottle.

What do you see happening?

Sam Poon

The science

The chemical reaction in this experiment (as well as the eggshell experiment, earlier in this chapter) is called an acid-base reaction. When you hear the word "acid," you may picture the scary stuff that burns your skin. While it's true that strong acids are very dangerous, weak acids are all around you and are quite safe. For example, the juice in lemons and limes is a weak acid, as is vinegar.

So what is a base? You can think of a base as sort of the opposite of an acid. Bases are often slippery, like soap. And it turns out that soap is a weak base. By now, you may have guessed that baking soda is also a weak base. (Strong bases, like strong acids, are dangerous).

When acids and bases come together, they react. In this case, (as with the eggshell experiment), the reactions produced the gas carbon dioxide, which floats up and goes into the balloon. Although you can't see gases, they still take up space, and all the tiny molecules of carbon dioxide fill up the balloon and blow it up

Going further

Try changing the amount of vinegar or baking soda you use. Does it change how much the balloon blows up?

Another classic science experiment uses baking soda and vinegar to model a volcano. In the figure, the kids put baking soda into the volcano and are about to pour vinegar (with red food dye) into the crater. What do you think will happen?!

CITRIC ACID AND BAKING SODA: ENDOTHERMIC REACTION

The preceding two experiments explore chemical reactions. In this one, you use baking soda and something called *citric acid,* which comes from citrus fruits (like lemons and limes), to see how some chemical reactions use heat.

Note: If you don't have citric acid, you can also explore endothermic reactions by mixing baking soda and vinegar, although the effect is less dramatic.

Supplies

Citric acid	Spoon
Baking soda	Lukewarm water
Bowl	

Instructions

1 **Put a few spoonfuls of baking soda in a bowl.**

I dyed my baking soda blue so that you can see the contrast with the citric acid, but you don't need to.

2 **Sprinkle citric acid onto your baking soda, as shown in the following figure.**

3 **Touch your lukewarm water and notice its temperature.**

Lukewarm means that the water isn't hot or cold.

4 **Pour some of this lukewarm water into your bowl, making sure to cover the areas with citric acid with water.**

What happened?

5 **Add more ingredients to your mixture to keep the reaction going.**

If adding water no longer causes a reaction, try sprinkling or more citric acid or add extra baking soda.

6 **Once you have a nice bubbly reaction going, touch it with your fingers.**

Has the temperature changed?

Please do not place your hands in your eyes. Citric acid, like lemon juice, will irritate your eyes.

Sam Poo

The science

An important part of chemical reactions is that they either use heat or give off heat. When citric acid and baking soda react, they use heat. The type of reaction that uses heat is called *endothermic*

As the citric acid and baking soda react, they are using the heat that is in the air around them. As they use up the heat, the space around the reaction gets cold.

You may wonder what would happen if there were absolutely no heat. The reaction would not take place! But it would have to be very, very, very cold.

Going further

Citric acid and baking soda are the ingredients used in bath bombs. Try looking up recipes online to make your own bath bomb. Mixing baking soda and vinegar will also give you an endothermic reaction Do you notice whether one mixture becomes noticeably colder?

YEAST AND THE STUFF IN THAT BROWN BOTTLE: EXOTHERMIC REACTION

In the preceding experiment, you can make a reaction that uses heat. Here, you create an *exothermic reaction*, which *creates* heat. To do this, you use yeast and hydrogen peroxide.

Yeast is a fungus; each individual yeast is one cell, like bacteria. Yeast is often used in baking to help bread rise. Hydrogen peroxide is a chemical that can be used to bleach paper or get rid of germs. You can find both at the grocery store.

Three percent hydrogen peroxide can irritate skin, but is more or less safe to use. Still, I strongly suggest gloves and eye protection for this experiment.

Supplies

Dry active yeast (available at grocery store)

Hydrogen peroxide (3 percent from grocery store; newly opened bottle is best)

Plastic water bottle

Very warm water

Dish soap

Small dish

Spoon

Baking pan

Gloves

Eye protection

Funnel (optional)

Food coloring (optional)

Measuring cup

Instructions

1 **Wearing your gloves and safety glasses, pour 1/3 cup of hydrogen peroxide into your bottle.**

You can use a funnel, if available.

Sam Poon

2 **Add a good squeeze of dish soap to the bottle and swish it around a bit to mix it.**

3 **(Optional) Add a few drops of food coloring into your bottle.**

4 **With your spoon, mix 1 tablespoon of dry yeast in a small amount of very warm (but not painfully hot) water in your small dish.**

5 **If the yeast gets sticky and hard to mix, add a little more water.**

Don't worry if some of it is still clumpy.

6 **Make sure that your bottle is in your baking pan (to catch the foam) and pour the yeast-water mixture into the bottle.**

The reaction may take a moment to get started.
What happens?

7 **Touch the bottle and foam.**

I recommend gloves because the foam can be hot, but it is not unsafe.

What do you notice?

The science

Did you notice in this chemical reaction that your bottle and the foam were warm to the touch? That is because this reaction created heat! Reactions that create heat are called *exothermic reactions*

An obvious example of an exothermic reaction is when you light a match. The materials in the match head react with those in the strip that you strike it against, and you create fire, and heat.

All chemical reactions either use or create heat, and heat is basically energy. So all chemical reactions either use or create energy. (**Note:** You always need energy to start a reaction, but exothermic reactions create more energy than they use.)

Going further

For another exothermic reaction, look up the vinegar and steel wool experiment online and try it for yourself.

PROJECT 5 PLANTS AND ANIMALS

THIS CHAPTER FOCUSES ON STUFF THAT IS ALIVE. You are going to sprout some seeds, use seeds to make a goo, learn about human and animal body parts, and more.

INTRODUCTION TO THE LIVING STUFF

The study of plants and animals is called *biology,* and it keeps scientists busy. There is a huge amount of diversity among living things, with an estimated 300,000 known species of plants and almost 8 million species of animals! (Many of these species have not yet been identified.)

Despite this diversity, different plants or animals share many behaviors, structures, and processes. For example, many plants grow from seeds. As another example, animals use fat as a way to store energy and keep warm. However, not all plants grow from seeds (some grow from spores), and the fat levels in animals vary by a large degree.

As a scientist interested in living things, it will serve you well to pay attention to the similarities and differences you encounter in the subjects you study.

As a junior scientist, it can sometimes be hard to study your subject directly. For example, you may want to study how blubber helps keep a walrus warm, but good luck getting your hands on a walrus! To get around this problem, you can create models to represent different aspects of biology.

If you love plants and animals, you will never run out of new things to study and learn.

I hope you have a great time studying plants and animals as you do the experiments in this chapter!

SPROUT AN AVOCADO SEED

The fruit you buy in a grocery store once came from a plant. Sprout an avocado seed to see biology in action.

Supplies

Avocado

Table knife (not too sharp)

Clear plastic cup or glass

Key

4 toothpicks

An adult to help

Water

Cutting board

Instructions

1 **Place your avocado on a cutting board and carefully cut it open.**

Never hold the avocado in your hand while cutting. Avocados can be slippery, so cut carefully.

2 **Remove the pit with a spoon or your fingers (not a knife) and wipe the pit clean with a paper towel.**

3 **Start to remove the seed coat.**

The *seed coat* is the brown layer that surrounds the pit. You can remove it by scraping a key against the avocado pit.

Scrape in one spot until the brown layer starts to flake off.

4 **After you scrape off a small piece of the seed coat with your key, use a toothpick and your fingernails to remove more of it.**

You want to expose the ridge that runs around the avocado pit. The toothpick in the figure points out this ridge.

5 **Continue to peel off the seed coat until the entire ridge is exposed.**

6 **Figure out the top side (pointy) and root side (flatter) of the pit**

7 **Put the pointy side up and stick three equally spaced toothpicks into the avocado, tilting the toothpicks up a little bit.**

8 **Place the pit and toothpicks on your cup, pointier side up, as shown in the figure.**

Top

Sam Poon

9 **Fill the cup with water so that the bottom portion of the pit is covered.**

10 **Put the cup in a sunny spot.**

11 **Wait and check on the pit every day or few days.**

12 **Replace water when the water level gets too low.**

The seed will likely take time to visibly sprout, even weeks. Check the progress by paying attention to the crack at the bottom of pit. The crack will start to open the tiniest bit, and at first, you may think your eyes are playing tricks on you. But as the seed grows, the crack will grow wider and wider, as you can see in the figure. Eventually, the root will come out, and then the plant will emerge from the top of the pit. This experiment takes some patience, but it is worth it!

The science

Plants grow from seeds, and seeds need water to sprout and water and sunlight to grow. Soil is also important for plants to grow. It provides extra nutrients, a place for the roots to grow into, and a way to anchor the plant so that it doesn't fall over. However, seeds will grow without soil. You also likely observed that although the roots and stem grow rather slowly, the process of the seed sprouting and growing is strong enough to crack open the avocado pit.

Did you realize the avocado pit is not the seed? The seed is small and inside the pit, as shown in this figure.

Seed

Sam Poon

Going further

Can you get your avocado seed to sprout in soil? Will the seed grow if you do not place it in sunlight? What about in a dark room? Plant multiple seeds and keep track of how long they take to sprout. Do some grow faster than others?

GROW SEEDS IN A PLASTIC BAGGY

A classic experiment all students of science should do: Watch different types of seeds sprout using nothing but water and sunlight.

Supplies

Seeds — pick your favorites.

Paper towel(s)

Plastic baggy/baggies

Permanent marker

Water

Tape (optional)

Window in a sunny spot (optional)

1 **Pick your seeds.**

I had success with the following types of seeds: chia, flax, sunflower, green bean, corn, pea, and carrot. I purchased all the seeds, although you may find success with some seeds taken straight from fruits. I did not have success with basil seeds.

2 **Wet a piece of paper towel and squeeze it out so it's damp.**

Depending on how many seeds you're planting, you may need more than one paper towel.

3 **Place one or more seeds on your paper towel.**

With some seeds, especially larger ones, you may choose to place only one or two in a bag. For seeds like chia and flax, you can sprinkle several onto a paper towel.

4 **Label your plastic bag(s) with the name of the seeds you are using.**

5 Gently place the paper towel into the plastic baggy.

6 Tape the plastic bag to a sunny window, with the seeds facing the sun or place it flat in a sunny spot.

After two or more days, your seeds will begin to sprout. If you want, use a notebook to keep track of how many days each different seed takes to sprout.

The science

By putting your various seeds in water and sunlight, you allowed for them to germinate, or start growing. Gardeners often use this plastic baggy method to start germination of their plants before they plant them in the soil.

This experiment gives you a great opportunity to take note of the similarities and differences between different living things.

Going further

Experiment with your seeds. Will they sprout outside in the winter? In soil in an egg container?

I challenge you to think of more experiments you can do with your seeds.

THREE SEED GOO

See how some seeds absorb water and make a fun goo.

Supplies

Flax seeds	Spoon or fork
Basil seeds	Water
Chia seeds	Cornstarch
2 bowls	Food coloring (optional)

Instructions

Part I: Preparing the seeds

1 **Add 1 tablespoon + 1 teaspoon flax seeds, 1 tablespoon basil seeds, and 2 tablespoon chia seeds into one bowl.**

Sam Poon

2 **Repeat Step 1 for the second bowl; set this bowl aside.**

3 **Measure out ¼ cup of water.**

4 **Pour just enough water in the bowl from your ¼ cup to cover the seeds and stir with your spoon.**

Watch the seeds for the next few minutes as they absorb the water. Compare them to your dry seeds. What changes are occurring? (This is a mini-experiment within the big experiment.)

5 **After the seeds have absorbed all the water, add a little more water; repeat until the seeds no longer absorb more water.**

The seeds should be gooey but without excess water.

6 **Put your fingers in the bowl.**

What do the seeds feel like? Compare them to your bowl with dry seeds – what differences do you see?

Instructions

Part II: Making goo

1 **If you want to color your goo, add several drops of food coloring to your seeds and mix it in.**

2 **Measure out 1/4 cup of cornstarch and stir half of it into your seeds.**

3 **Add some more cornstarch and start to *knead* (push or mix) the cornstarch into the seeds with your hands, as shown in the figure.**

The cornstarch will seem to dissolve into the seeds.

 This step is messy! Do it in or over the bowl.

Sam Poor

4 **Continue to knead your goo until it no longer looks dusty.**

5 **Repeat Steps 3 and 4 until you've used the entire ¼ cup; if the cornstarch has fallen into your bowl, scoop it out and add it to your slime and knead again.**

The kneading may take a minute or two every time you add cornstarch, but consider it part of playing with the goo!

6 **If your goo is still sticking to your hands after the cornstarch is fully dissolved, add more cornstarch.**

Add about 1 extra tablespoon at a time and knead it in. I usually add an extra 2 to 3 tablespoons.

Once the mixture stops sticking to your hands, you're finished! Enjoy your goo.

Sometimes the goo becomes too firm and starts to dry out after playing with it for a while. If this happens, wet your hands and mash the water back into the goo. If it becomes very dried out, you can dip the whole thing in water and then dust it with extra cornstarch as you knead it again. Do you like your goo slimier or drier?

This slime is organic, and it will go bad. When you are done playing with it, seal it in a plastic baggie or container and place in the fridge. Throw it out after a few days unless you want a whole different type of science experiment!

Sam Poon

The science

All seeds need water to grow and different types of seeds have different ways to make sure that they get enough water. The flax, chia, and basil seeds all swell up and create a gel around them when placed in water. This gel allows them to make sure that they have the water they need to grow. When these seeds are mixed with cornstarch, a unique material is created.

Going further

Compare these seeds to other types of seeds. Would an apple or pear seed get bigger in water? Can you think of a synthetic (man-made) material that absorbs a lot of water? What about diapers?

HOW MUCH SUGAR?

Your body does need a little bit of sugar, but many foods have way too much sugar. Find out how much sugar is too much in this eye-opening experiment.

Supplies

Kitchen scale or measuring spoons

Sugar

Spoon

2 or more equal size bowls (smaller is better)

Nutrition labels from a few foods and drinks

Instructions

1 Find some foods and drinks with nutrition labels.

Nutrition labels are found on almost any food you buy in a box or bottle. They tell you what is in the food.

2 Pick an amount of sugar to weigh between 25 grams.

Preteens are supposed to have no more than 15 to 25 grams of sugar a day! You are going to find out what that looks like.

3 If you are using a scale, put your bowl on it and press tare.

Pressing tare makes the scale say 0 so that you weigh only your sugar and not the bowl.

4 Make sure that your units are on grams or g (not oz).

If you are using measuring spoons, use these numbers:

  » 1 teaspoon is a little over 4 grams of sugar

  » 1 tablespoon is about 14 grams of sugar

5 **Add sugar to the bowl until you reach the number of grams you picked in Step 2.**

If you picked 15 grams and are using measuring spoons, add a little more than 1 tablespoon. Don't worry about being exact.

Sam Poon

6 **Look at the sugar in your bowl.**

Does it look like a lot? That is the maximum amount of extra sugar you should have in an entire day.

7 **Pick one of your foods or drinks from Step 1 and read the nutrition label.**

How many grams of sugar are in one serving of your food? Use the figure to guide you.

2.5 servings per container x 31 grams of sugar per serving = 77 grams of sugar in a bottle!

High fructose corn syrup = sugar

Sam Poon

8 Check your serving size.

The nutrition label in the figure is from a popular 20-ounce soft drink, and it has 2.5 servings in a single bottle!

9 Measure out the amount of sugar in your food or drink as you did in Step 5.

Look at your bowl. Is there a lot of sugar in it? Is it more or less sugar than your first bowl?

10 Repeat Steps 7 to 9 for the rest of your food and drinks.

The science

Humans evolved to like sugar because sugar provides energy, and in the old days, it was hard to find! Fruits and milks have sugars in them, and these foods are good for you.

The problem is, food companies dump tons of sugar into their foods to make them taste good. But this makes us eat too much sugar, which can make us sick and unhealthy.

Sometimes the ingredient list of a food won't say sugar but will say high fructose corn syrup, which is a type of sugar that some nutritionists argue is worse than other types.

Going further

Start learning to read the nutrition labels of foods so that you can make good choices about what you put into your body. Learn about proteins, fiber, and fat. However, some of the best foods, such as fruits and vegetables, come without nutrition labels!

TASTE BUD DETECTION

Are you a picky eater? Use food coloring to study the taste buds on your tongue and find out whether you are a supertaster!

Supplies

Blue food coloring

Cotton swab

Mirror

Small piece of paper (1 inch x 1 inch is fine)

Hole punch (standard size)

Drinking water

Instructions

1 **Punch a hole in your piece of paper and set it aside.**

2 **Put a drop of blue food coloring on your cotton swab and rub it onto your tongue.**

Make sure that you get the sides and front of the tongue (where the most taste buds are).

3 Swish some water around your mouth so that the dye isn't on too thick.

The dye will stain most of your tongue blue, but your taste buds will remain a whitish-pink. Identify some taste buds in the mirror.

4 Put your hole-punched paper onto your tongue, as shown in the figure.

5 Count how many taste buds you have inside the circle (or have a friend count for you) and write down your number.

6 Test a few different areas on your tongue, including the front and sides.

In adults, research found that those with more than 35 taste buds inside the circle were *supertasters.* Those with 15 to 35 taste buds were average, and those with less than 15 tastebuds inside the circle were called nontasters. How many taste buds do you have?

The science

There may be a reason some people hate broccoli! Some people are born with more taste buds than others. The people with lots of taste buds are known as supertasters. Supertasters tend to taste bitter foods, like broccoli or coffee, more strongly.

Going further

It turns out that children often tend to taste bitter foods more strongly than adults. The research about supertasters was done on adults. Maybe you can do your own experiment to find out whether kids who have more taste buds are picky eaters!

FAT KEEPS YOU WARM

You may live in a place with a cold winter, but can you imagine actually living in the Arctic Ocean? It would be so cold, yet for many animals, the freezing cold water is their home. These animals have generally adapted by evolving a lot, and I mean a lot, of blubber, or fat. See how fat protects you from the cold in this experiment.

Supplies

Shortening, like Crisco	Water
Large mixing bowl	Ice

1 **Pour (cold) water and ice into your bowl, but don't fill it completely.**

2 **Cover your hand in shortening.**

You may want help for this! You want a layer about ½ to 1 inch thick.

3 **Take time to make sure there are no cracks in your "blubber layer" that water could get into.**

It can be a little tricky to get your hand fully covered, so a parent or friend may be helpful here.

4 **Put your bare hand into the ice water (brrr!) and take it out.**

5 **Put your "blubber hand" in the ice water.**

What does it feel like?

Sam Poon

The science

Animals adapt to be able to survive in their environment. For example, fish live underwater, so they evolved body parts that help them breathe underwater. In contrast, humans live on land and can't breathe underwater at all! Giraffes evolved long necks to eat leaves off trees, and sharks evolved sharp teeth that allow them to chew the fish they hunt and capture. (The adaptation and evolution I am talking about does not happen in an animal's lifetime, but usually over the course of hundreds of thousands of years.)

Animals that live in cold climates had to evolve a way to survive the cold. Animals like walruses and seals evolved lots and lots of blubber that could keep the important organs inside of them warm!

Going further

Look at more animals (in person or pictures) and think about the adaptations they have. Think about even the simple things. Where are their eyes placed? What is the shape of their nose? Are their teeth sharp or flat, or do they even have teeth? Look at some pictures of insects; their adaptations can get really crazy!

PROJECT **6** PERCEIVING IS BELIEVING

YOUR SENSES TAKE IN INFORMATION ABOUT THE WORLD AROUND YOU AND GIVE YOU THE ABILITY TO NAVIGATE THAT WORLD. The five traditional senses are seeing, smelling, hearing, tasting, and feeling. However, sometimes your senses are not quite reliable. In this chapter, you trick your senses to start to learn how your brain interprets the information it receives.

IT'S ALL IN YOUR HEAD

One of the coolest facts to realize is that although you use your eyes, ears, nose, skin, and more to sense the environment, it is your brain that is necessary to perceive every image, sound, smell, taste, and sensation you have.

Your brain, along with your spinal cord, is made up of special cells called *neurons*. These neurons send out long projections to all the parts of your body; these projections are called *nerves*. The nerves carry information to and from various parts of your body. It is the nerves that tell your brain if you have a pain in your hand or if a particular odor has entered your nose. The nerves carry very important information, but ultimately it is your brain that controls everything you perceive.

For example, you obviously use your eyes to see, but it is the brain that processes these images. If the connection between your eyes and brain were cut, you would see nothing, even if the eyes themselves were fully functioning. Damage to parts of the brain that are important for processing vision (such as the occipital cortex) can actually make you go blind, even if your eyes still work.

Another example of the incredible power of our brain comes from studying something called *phantom limb syndrome.* Sometimes people who have lost a limb continue to feel pain in the limb they have lost. Yes, that's right, people can feel pain in body parts that they no longer have. How is this possible?

Phantom limb syndrome is possible because it is your brain that processes pain and tells you where that pain is coming from. If you slam your hand in a door, your nerves carry information to your spinal cord and brain (the *nervous system)* that tell your brain "pain in hand." After you get that signal, you experience, or perceive, a "pain in hand." But even if you have lost a hand, the nerves that went from your hand to the brain still exist (although they are shorter and damaged). These nerves can misfire and tell your brain the hand is still there and that it hurts. (While phantom limb syndrome is an interesting case of how the brain works, it is an extremely frustrating and uncomfortable condition for those who experience it.) It turns out that everything you experience, is indeed, "all in your head."

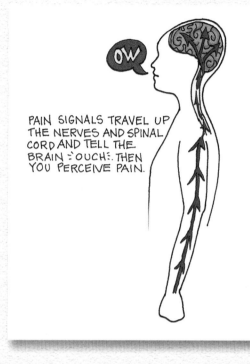

Your brain evolved to accurately identify the things around you so that you can successfully interact with and survive in your environment. However, as you will see in this chapter, the brain can sometimes get things wrong, and can be tricked. Tricking your brain is an excellent way to start to understand how it works. As you go through this chapter, be willing to be amazed as you investigate how your senses interact with that mysterious gray material inside your skull!

JELLY BEAN TASTE TEST

You learned that you smell with your nose and taste with your tongue, but would you believe me if I told you that you also taste with your nose?

Supplies

One or more jelly beans

Instructions

1 Plug your nose with one hand and pick up a jelly bean with the other.

Make sure that your nose is plugged really well.

2 With your nose plugged, put the jelly bean in your mouth and start to chew.

Think about the flavor you are tasting. Get the jelly bean nice and chewed, but don't swallow

3 Without swallowing, let go of (unplug) your nose.

What happened?

This experiment won't work if you have a cold. Do you know why?

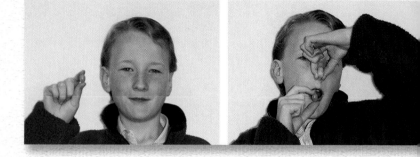

The science

It turns out that you not only taste with your tongue, you taste with your nose as well! But how can this be? It's not like you chew with your nose.

Well, if you have ever laughed really hard while drinking and spit water out of your nose, you'll know that your mouth and nose are connected. While you chew, air is actually being pushed up from your mouth and into your nose, and that air carries little tiny pieces of the food you are chewing. Your nose then sends a signal to your brain that helps you perceive (or experience) the flavor of the food. When you plug your nose, you block that signal and get the taste signals only from your tongue, and the food tastes blander. This is also why food tastes bland when you have a cold!

Going further

Experiment with other foods. Can you block the taste by holding your nose? Give a blindfolded jelly bean taste test to your friends and see whether they can guess the flavor of the jelly beans (without seeing them first) while holding their noses.

WHERE'S THAT SOUND?

Try to trick your friend and learn how the brain locates sounds.

Supplies

A set of keys or something else small that makes noise

Blindfold

Another person

Chair

Ear plug (optional)

Instructions

1 Have the other person sit in the chair and blindfold her.

Make sure she doesn't peek!

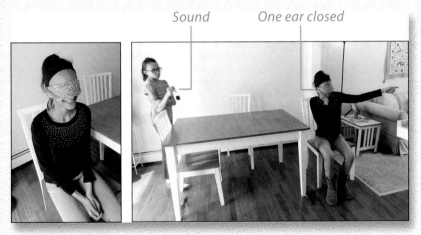

Sound   One ear closed

2 Move around the person quietly, at times stopping to jingle your keys (or other noisy item) and asking her to point to where she thinks the sound is coming from.

Try at least five different spots. Try one directly in front of her head and one directly behind her head. How many times did she correctly point to the location of the keys?

3 **Ask the other person to plug one ear using an earplug or a finger to block sound.**

Make sure that the ear is really plugged, or the experiment won't work!

4 **Repeat Step 2.**

Make sure that you jingle the keys on both sides of the other person's head several times. Try directly in front of and behind her head as well. How did the other person do with one ear plugged?

The science

Most likely you found that the other person could correctly point to the location of the keys when both ears were unplugged, but had some trouble once he or she plugged an ear! So why does plugging an ear make it hard to locate sound?

The way your brain is able locate sounds is by figuring out the difference in timing and loudness of the sound in each ear.

For example, if a sound comes directly from the right of your head, it's going to reach your right ear a lot sooner than it reaches your left ear. It will also be louder in the right ear. Once the sound reaches each ear, the ear will talk to the brain. The brain uses the timing and loudness differences to figure out where the sound is coming from.

Going further

Take earplugs and plug both ears, but use a sound loud enough that your subject can still hear it. Can he identify the sound with hearing muffled in two ears?

POKE YOUR FRIEND IN THE NAME OF SCIENCE

Your skin covers your whole body. But is all skin created equal when it comes to touching? Do this experiment to find out.

Supplies

Cardboard

Toothpicks

Duct tape or other strong tape

Blindfold

Another person

Instructions

1 Cut out three small pieces of cardboard.

My cardboard was about 1.5 x 3 inches.

2 On one piece of cardboard, tape one toothpick, as shown in the figure.

3 On the second piece of cardboard, tape two toothpicks 2 to 4 mm apart.

Press your finger against the tips of the toothpicks to make sure that they're lined up with each other perfectly.

4 On the final piece of cardboard, tape two toothpicks 8 mm or more apart, lining up the tips of the toothpicks.

5 **Ask the other person to sit down and blindfold her.**

The other person is your *subject*. (The subject is the person you are doing the experimenting on.)

6 **Have your subject put one forearm on the table, with the underside up (palm up).**

7 **Gently poke your subject's forearm with one of your toothpick contraptions, as shown in the figure, but do not tell them which one you're using.**

Make sure both toothpicks touch the arm at the exact same time. If you touch the arm unevenly, the experiment won't work.

Please poke gently so that you don't hurt your subject.

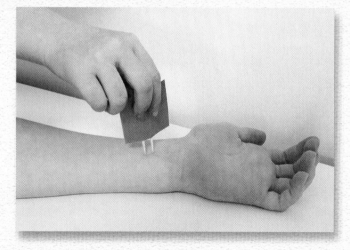

8 **Ask your subject to tell you whether she thinks you used one or two toothpicks to poke.**

If you want, record the data.

9 Poke your subject one or more times each with the other toothpick contraptions.

You can try to trick her by using the same contraption twice in a row.

10 Repeat Steps 7 to 9 but this time poke the pad of the subject's index finger instead of her forearm.

Record the data, if you want. What did you find?

The science

You may have discovered that when you poked the forearm, but not the fingertips, your subject had trouble telling how many toothpicks you were using. Why is this?

Everything you perceive is controlled by your brain, and signals that you have been touched travel up your nerves (which are made of nerve cells). In your fingertips, two pokes close together will stimulate signals to be sent up two different nerve cells, so your brain will be able to say, "Hey, I'm getting two inputs down there!" However, your forearm is much less sensitive and has fewer nerve endings. In the forearm, two pokes close together will often send a signal up only one nerve cell. Because your brain is getting only one signal, it incorrectly thinks your forearm is getting one poke!

Going further

Test other regions of your body. How sensitive is your back, your calf, or your toe? If you want to do a quick demonstration of this concept but don't have your toothpicks, try using one or two fingers on a friend's back over their shirt.

Do not poke near the person's face.

THE WATER IS WARM – NO COLD – NO . . . .

If you've ever jumped into the ocean, lake, or pool, you may have noticed the water felt very cold at first but then eventually felt comfortable! This is because your perception of temperature can be relative. Explore this phenomenon in this cool (or should I say hot?) experiment.

Supplies

3 bowls large enough to fit your hand inside

Very warm water

Lukewarm water

Cold water plus ice cubes

Timer

Instructions

1 Place your three bowls in a row, with the largest bowl in the middle.

2 Fill the middle bowl with room temperature water.

You will be putting your hands in the bowl so don't fill the bowl all the way to the top. You don't want the water to overflow.

3 Put ice water in one of the other bowls, again leaving room at the top.

4 Put your very warm water in the last bowl.

The water should not be painful to the touch. You can get very warm water from the tap or have an adult help you heat a little bit of water until it is warm, not hot.

5 Place one hand in the ice water bowl and one hand in the very warm water bowl, as shown in the figure, leaving your hands in the water for 45 to 60 seconds.

If the cold of the ice water becomes painful, remove your hand. Do not leave your hand in the ice water for too long.

Room temperature
Very warm   Ice cold

6 Remove your hands from the bowls.

7 Place your right hand in the middle bowl with the room temperature water.

Does the water feel cold or warm?

8 Take your right hand out and put your left hand into the middle bowl with the room temperature water.

Does the water feel hot or cold?

9 Continue to switch your hands back and forth in the middle bowl, paying attention to how warm or cold the water feels.

10 Put both hands in at once.

What do you notice?

The science

Did you notice that the room temperature water felt warm on the ice water hand and cool on the warm water hand? This is because of something called sensory adaptation. (This is different than the adaptation of evolution).

There are nerve cells in your hands that respond to cold and nerves that respond to heat. If you put your hand in ice water, the "cold" nerve cells will get activated, and the "hot" nerve cells will shut down. But if you leave your hand in ice water for a while, the "cold" nerve cells adapt, meaning they don't respond as much! If you now move your hand from the ice water to the warmer water, the "cold" nerve cells are basically shut off, but the "hot" nerve cells actually respond more than they would have had they not been deactivated by the ice water. This makes you perceive that the water is warmer than it really is. (The opposite happens when you move your hand from warm to cold water). If the temperature is too extreme, however, you'll never adapt.

Adaptation occurs for lots of sensory inputs and is necessary to help you ignore unimportant stimuli, like the sensation of clothes against your skin.

Going further

Test visual adaptation. Go into a dark room and wait 10 to 15 minutes with no lights and no phones (maybe play some music) and notice your visual ability. Now quickly turn the light on and off. What happened? Did your eyes adapt to the dark?

THE PENNY CHALLENGE

Are two eyes better than one? Find out how your depth perception changes when you blindfold one eye.

Supplies

Blindfold or scarf (to go over one eye)

2 pennies

Instructions

1 Place one penny in each hand between your thumb and index finger.

2 Stand or sit with your arms straight out a little wider than your shoulders, bend your elbows a teeny tiny bit, and hold the pennies so that the edges of the pennies are facing each other, as in the figure.

3 Move the two pennies toward each other and try to touch the edges of the pennies together on the first try.

4 Repeat Steps 1 through 3 a few times.

   How many times did you touch the pennies together on the first try? If not they didn't touch on first try, were you close?

5 Cover one eye with a blindfold and repeat Steps 1 through 4.

   What did you find?

The science

You may have found that this task was a little challenging with no blindfold and really challenging with one eye covered. This is because you need both your eyes to get true 3-D vision. (Scientists call 3-D vision stereopsis.)

Each of your eyes gets a slightly different image of the world. Each eye then sends its image information to the brain, and the brain compares the differences between the two images it's receiving. This comparison lets the brain know how close or far away things are and where they are in space.

If one eye is blocked, the world looks kind of flat, like a picture, and it's difficult to tell exactly how far away something is. When you try to touch the edges of the pennies together with one eye covered, your brain doesn't have enough information to do the task successfully.

Going further

Try other tasks that test your 3D vision. Try dropping pennies int condiment cups or throwing ping pong balls into cups with water. How do you do with one eye closed? Can you think of you own 3D vision test?

ROJECT 7 ART AND SCIENCE

Sam Poon

SCIENCE AND ART MAY SEEM LIKE THEY ARE WORLDS APART, BUT IN MANY WAYS, THEY ARE INTERTWINED. Scientists often have to draw and record what they see, and indeed, early scientists made beautiful drawings of items like a new plant they discovered or the insides of a bacterial cell. Artists also often find inspiration from nature and from advances in science and technology. Artists who build sculptures or other 3-D creations have to use engineering to understand how to put things together. (Engineering is building or creating new things and figuring out how to make things work).

Scientists and artists both use creativity in their projects. In this chapter, I suggest several ideas for combining art and science, but the possibilities are endless! I encourage you to explore mixing science and art as you continue on your journey to build new creations and learn about different aspects of our world.

DELICIOUS SMELLING PAINT

An important part of being a scientist is coming up with new ways to use materials. You might be familiar with the flavored powder packets from the grocery store which you can mix with water to make sugar drinks. The powders in these packets are dyed different colors; you can take advantage of the dye to make your own paints. You will be creating a multi-sensory art project that you can both see **and** smell!

Supplies

Drink mix packets, such as Kool-Aid, 0.13 oz

Small bowls

Spoon

Water

Watercolor paper or white construction paper

Paintbrushes

Instructions

1   **Pour out each drink mix packet into a small bowl.**

2   **Mix 1 to 2 tablespoons of water in with the powder in each bowl using your spoon.**

3   **Paint!**

My artist created an elephant, but you can also make something smelly, like a strawberry or lemon, with your smelly paints.

The science

In addition to paints, dyes are used to color food, like powder drink packets. You repurposed dye, which was originally intended to make drinks look appealing, to instead create art.

Going further

What other materials can you use for a different purpose than they were originally intended? You also can use this activity to explore color mixing. In the figure, you can see the artist mixed the primary colors of blue, red, and yellow to create orange, green, purple, and brown.

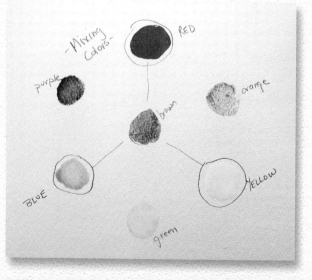

SHAVING CREAM PATTERNS

Combine food coloring and shaving cream to explore materials which attract and repel water, while making unique prints.

Supplies

White cardstock or index cards

Liquid food coloring

Flat dish like a baking pan or plate

Shaving cream (the white foamy type)

Chopstick (for larger sizes) or toothpick (for smaller prints)

Ruler or something with a long flat edge

Instructions

1 Decide how big you would like your prints to be.

The artist used a full sheet of paper, but you can cut your paper smaller or use the back of white index cards.

2 Create a layer of shaving cream on your flat dish.

The shaving cream layer should be larger than your paper.

3 Place several drops of food coloring on the shaving cream, as shown in the figure.

4 Run your chopstick or toothpick through the shaving cream in order to swirl the food coloring and create a design, as shown in the figure.

5 Place your paper on top of the shaving cream and press down.

6 **Pull off your paper and scrape off the shaving cream using the flat edge of your ruler, as shown in the figure.**

How did your pattern come out?

The science

You may have noticed that the pattern on your card and the pattern on your shaving cream looked a little different. This is because of the way the food coloring interacted with each material.

Some materials, like cotton or sponges, are attracted to water. These materials are *hydrophilic*.

Other materials, like glass or plastic, repel water. These materials are *hydrophobic*.

Paper is hydrophilic, and food coloring is made mostly of water. Therefore, the food coloring was attracted to, and dyed, the paper.

Shaving cream, on the other hand, is partly hydrophobic and partly hydrophilic. The hydrophilic parts of the food dye absorb into the shaving cream, but the hydrophobic parts trap the food coloring so that it doesn't spread around. Did you notice your dye stayed in one place when you added it to the shaving cream?

Going further

Add food coloring to the shaving cream and then spray it with water. What happens? Can you find other hydrophilic and hydrophobic materials in your house?

TWO PICTURES BECOME ONE

Learn about how your visual system processes images while creating a simple, classic toy, called a *thaumatrope*.

Supplies

White cardstock

Scissors

Two rubber bands or cotton twine

Colored pencils or markers

Glue stick

Hole punch

Cup with large round bottom

Instructions

1 **Use the bottom of a cup to help you trace three circles onto white cardstock.**

My circles are 3 inches in diameter.

2 **Pick a circle to be your practice circle and draw a simple design in it that has two or more components, as shown in the figure.**

For example, our artist's drawing has a boat, a sun, and an ocean.

3 **Cut out the remaining two circles.**

4 **Divide your drawing into two parts.**

In the artist's drawing the sun and ocean is one part, and the boat is the other.

5 **Draw one part of your design in each of the two circles, as shown in the figure.**

Note that one of the drawings is upside down in the example.

The trick here is to line up your designs so that if you put them on top of each other, they would be one complete picture.

6 **Glue the circles together with the designs facing out, but with one of the images upside down.**

You can see the correct orientation for gluing them together in the figure.

Upside down

7 Punch a hole in each side of the circle.

8 Loop your rubber bands through the hole, as in the figure.

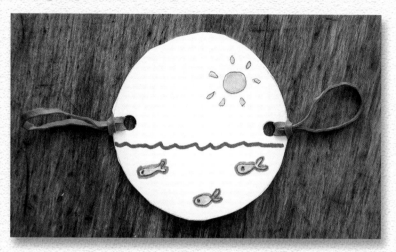

9 Pick up one rubber band in each hand and twist them using your thumb and index finger so that the disc quickly spins around.

What do you see?

The science

When you spun the disc around quickly, you should have found that the two images blurred together and appeared to be a single picture. Why does this happen?

First, it's helpful to know that light enters your pupil (the black part in the center of your eye) and then travels to the back of the eye, hitting an area called the *retina*. The retina then sends signals to your brain about the image, and you then perceive the image.

It turns out that you perceive each image for a fraction of a second longer than (the light from) each image is actually on the retina. When you spin your disc fast enough, your brain holds onto the two individual images on each side of the disc and perceives them as one single image!

Going further

Explore other drawings and images you can make. How big can you make the thaumatrope and still retain the desired effect? If you are feeling adventurous, look up online how to create "zoetrope" and use the principles you explored in this project to create an actual animation.

MAGNET MONSTERS

There are so many ways to use magnets. In this experiment, you use magnets to make awesome creatures with mix-and-match parts. You can use lots of recycled items found around the house. This project combines science, art, and engineering.

Supplies

Permanent marker

4 to 6 donut magnets

Small empty box (for example, a box that contained a bar of soap)

Construction paper

Glue gun (low heat)

Tacky glue or glue stick

Recycled household materials for decoration –for example, twist ties, lids from plastic bottles, buttons

Craft store decorations (optional) — for example, pipe cleaners, googly eyes, or beads

Instructions

Part I: Marking Magnets

1 Put all your magnets in a stack.

It is very important to you mark your magnets to identify the *poles*. Every magnet has what is called a north pole and a south pole. Two north poles (or two south poles) will push against each other, or repel. But a north and south pole will stick together.

2 Use your permanent marker to make an *X* on the top magnet, as shown in the figure.

3 Remove the magnet from the stack.

Do not flip over your stack.

4 Place an *X* on the top of the next magnet in the stack, as shown in the figure; repeat for all magnets.

5 Restack your magnets to double-check that the *X* is on the top side of all your magnets.

Sam Poor

Instructions

Part II: Making your Monster

1 Cut out pieces of construction paper the same size as your box and glue them to your box to create the base for your monsters.

My monsters are green and purple. Be creative! You can make a striped or polka-dotted monster, if you want.

2 Determine which side of the box is the front or "face" of your monster.

3 Determine how many magnet spots you want and where.

Magnet spots are where your magnet appendages will go. Make sure to balance the magnets so your creature won't fall over! This is engineering! Use the figure as a guide.

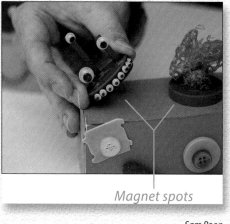

Magnet spots

Sam Poon

You are going to glue magnets on the inside of your monster box in your magnet spots.

4 Open your box; have an adult help you with the glue gun and place glue on the blank side of your magnet.

Glue gun glue dries quickly, so you need to work quickly.

 Glue gun glue can be extremely hot, especially if you're not working with a low heat gun.

5 Place the magnet inside the box in your magnet spot with the blank side touching the box.

Magnets glued inside the box

6 **Repeat Steps 4 and 5 for all your magnet spots.**

Make sure that you have magnets left to use as outside magnets.

7 **Place (don't glue) your outside magnets onto your magnet spots.**

The blank side should be facing up, and the X-marked side should be facing down.

8 **Glue your decorations directly onto your box.**

Be creative!

Make sure you do not glue things onto your magnet spots.

9 **Use a glue gun or tacky glue to attach whatever you desire onto the blank sides of your magnets.**

For one monster, for example, I put black pipe cleaners on one magnet and straws with googly eyes onto another magnet.

10 **Once your glue has dried, place your magnet appendages onto your magnet spots, mixing and matching them and moving them around.**

As long as you have more magnets, you can always make more magnet appendages. Just make sure to put the glue on the right side of the magnet!

Sam Poon

The science

Magnets are fun and can also be useful! In this activity, you used magnets to create a toy. As you engineered your creation, you had to be careful to keep track of the poles of each magnet. If you had placed the magnet in the wrong orientation (the wrong way), your inside and outside magnets would have repelled each other, and you would not have been able to attach your magnet appendages.

Magnetic poles are named north and south because the north pole of the magnet inside a compass points to the north pole, and the south pole of the magnet points to the south pole. These poles are responsible for the direction of the magnetic field. North and south poles are attracted to each other, but two north poles or two south poles will repel each other.

Going further

Discover other creative uses for magnets around your house. Can you use them to pick up dropped paperclips or nails? Can you find any magnets in your house or school that are being used in a functional way?

ABOUT THE AUTHOR

Olivia Mullins is the founder of Science Delivered, a San Diego based nonprofit that specializes in hands-on science enrichment for elementary and middle-school students. She believes an understanding and enjoyment of science enriches the lives of both kids and adults.

Prior to Science Delivered, Dr. Mullins worked in research as a Neuroscientist for nine years, obtaining her PhD along the way. During this time, she enjoyed both research and outreach and found she had a knack for distilling complex subjects into digestible pieces of information. She has a passion for teaching students from all backgrounds and expanding equal access to education.

DEDICATION

For all the children who love to laugh and learn.

AUTHOR'S ACKNOWLEDGMENTS

First I must acknowledge my husband Simon Mushi who is endlessly tolerant of my turning our kitchen and dining room into a kid's science lab. Thank you for your support of my endeavors and the extra work you put in while I was writing this book.

A big thank you to talented Sam Poon who contributed the majority of pictures in this book and was a pleasure to work with. Another big thank you to my mom, artist Cynthia Mullins, who created and photographed most of the art projects, sometimes twice, and helped with photo editing. I love you! Thank you to my other photographers, Orianna Helms and Amanda Flachsbart, for sending over takes and retakes and lending us your kids' images. Thank you to our awesome models Anika Pitts, Avery Pitts, and Teke Helms (and hand model Georgia Helms).

Thank you to Kelly Ewing and Amy Fandrei for all your help and advice and to the rest of the people at Wiley for this amazing opportunity. Thank you to Elizabeth Kurtzman for your awesome illustrations. Thank you to Lindsey Handley for the recommendation that started all this.

Paul Bonthuis and Charlie Toft, thank your for your careful and thorough technical editing and responses to multiple queries. Carter Ewing, thank you for testing all of the experiments and for your helpful feedback!

Stephanie Mullins, thank you for the vital and ongoing help with photo editing — and during your maternity leave no less! This book, and creating Science Delivered, would have been a lot harder without you. Thank you to Oliver Mullins for the support and chemistry explanations. Clinton Mullins, you've been very supportive of Science Delivered, so thank you for that.

Thank you to the kids in our Science Delivered classes who are so incredibly curious, fun, loving, and inspiring. You've made me so happy I chose this path.

Finally, I'd like to acknowledge my son Isaac Estomih Mullins Mushi — you are only two and didn't do anything for the book, but I have to say I love you a whole lot.

PUBLISHER'S ACKNOWLEDGMENTS

Senior Acquisitions Editor: Amy Fandrei

Project Editor: Kelly Ewing

Copy Editor: Kelly Ewing

Editorial Assistant: Kayla Hoffman

Sr. Editorial Assistant: Cherie Case

Illustrator: Elizabeth Kurtzman

Photographers: Sam Poon, Amanda Flachsbart, Cynthia Mullins, Orianna Helms

Reviewers: Paul J. Bonthuis, PhD Charles J. Cavanaugh Toft, Carter Ewing

Production Editor: Tamilmani Varadharaj